God's Trail of Tears

Ellen Crosby

Illustrated by Max Stasiuk

Copyright © 2011, 2023 Ellen Crosby
Copyright © 2011, 2023 TEACH Services, Inc.
ISBN-13: 978-1-4796-1691-6 (Paperback)
ISBN-13: 978-1-4796-1692-3 (ePub)
Library of Congress Control Number: 2023933683

TEACH Services, Inc.
PUBLISHING
www.TEACHServices.com • (800) 367-1844

Many moons ago, three Great Persons left their home in Orion and traveled to Earth. They came to create a new world; They had chosen Earth in the Milky Way galaxy. Earth was dark and empty and covered with deep water. There were no fish in the water. There was not even any air to breathe.

The three Great Persons were the Father, the Son, and the Holy Spirit—They made up the God family.

The first day of Creation started when God spoke, "Let there be light!" Beautiful light flooded the Earth and danced across the waters. It sparkled like millions of diamonds. God looked over the world bathed in light, and He was very pleased.

The next day God made the air. He put some of the water above the Earth where He made clouds in many different kinds of shapes. He made the wind in mighty jet streams blowing high in the sky. He made the soft breezes as well. God felt the soft breezes touching His face, and He took a deep breath of the new air. It was very good air.

On the third day God spoke, "Let the dry land appear!" The water rushed away into seas, rivers, and gurgling streams. Trees, grass, and flowers suddenly appeared.

The three Great Persons took a walk through the woods and looked at the trees. They walked into a meadow and picked some strawberries. They tasted the berries and smiled. They tasted very good!

On the fourth day God made the mighty sun to shine in the daytime and the moon to light the night. The three Great Persons walked along the seashore and felt the warmth of the sun on Their backs. They noticed how warm the sand felt to Their bare feet. They waded into the water to see how cool it felt. At evening They looked up to see the light of home shining from Orion, and They pulled down the waving blue and green curtains of the northern lights. They were happy with Their work, and They all agreed, "This is good!"

On the fifth day of Creation, God said, "Let the waters bring forth their moving creatures and the birds that fly above the Earth."
In the seas appeared whales, porpoises, and fish of every kind. Birds flew about and sang the songs that God had given them.

God fed the fish and put out food for the birds. He told them to start having families of their own. The three Great Persons took a walk and saw the birds busy making nests and singing happily.

At the end of the day the birds became quieter, and a Whip-poor-will bird sang his evening song in the nearby hills. The three Great Persons listened and were very pleased.

On the sixth day God said, "Let the Earth bring forth cattle and beasts and creeping things." Suddenly, horses, cows, sheep, goats, dogs, cats, lions, elephants, moose, deer, rabbits, chipmunks, caterpillars, ladybugs, and many more animals appeared. God showed the animals what they could eat. He told the animals He wanted them to have babies and make homes for them. The animals spread out, looking for the right place to make their homes. Each animal chose a place that was best for them. The three Great Persons were so pleased!

It was God's greatest wish to have people on Earth, and They couldn't wait any longer. They looked at each other and said, "Let us make man in Our likeness."

God took some clay and formed a man with it. When the man was completely finished, He breathed His own breath of life into the man's nostrils, and the man's heart began beating, he started breathing, and he woke up!

God made a beautiful garden home for Adam and Eve and named it Eden. It had delightful gardens complete with rivers, trees, and a lovely path to walk on. It had magnificent gates at the entrance.

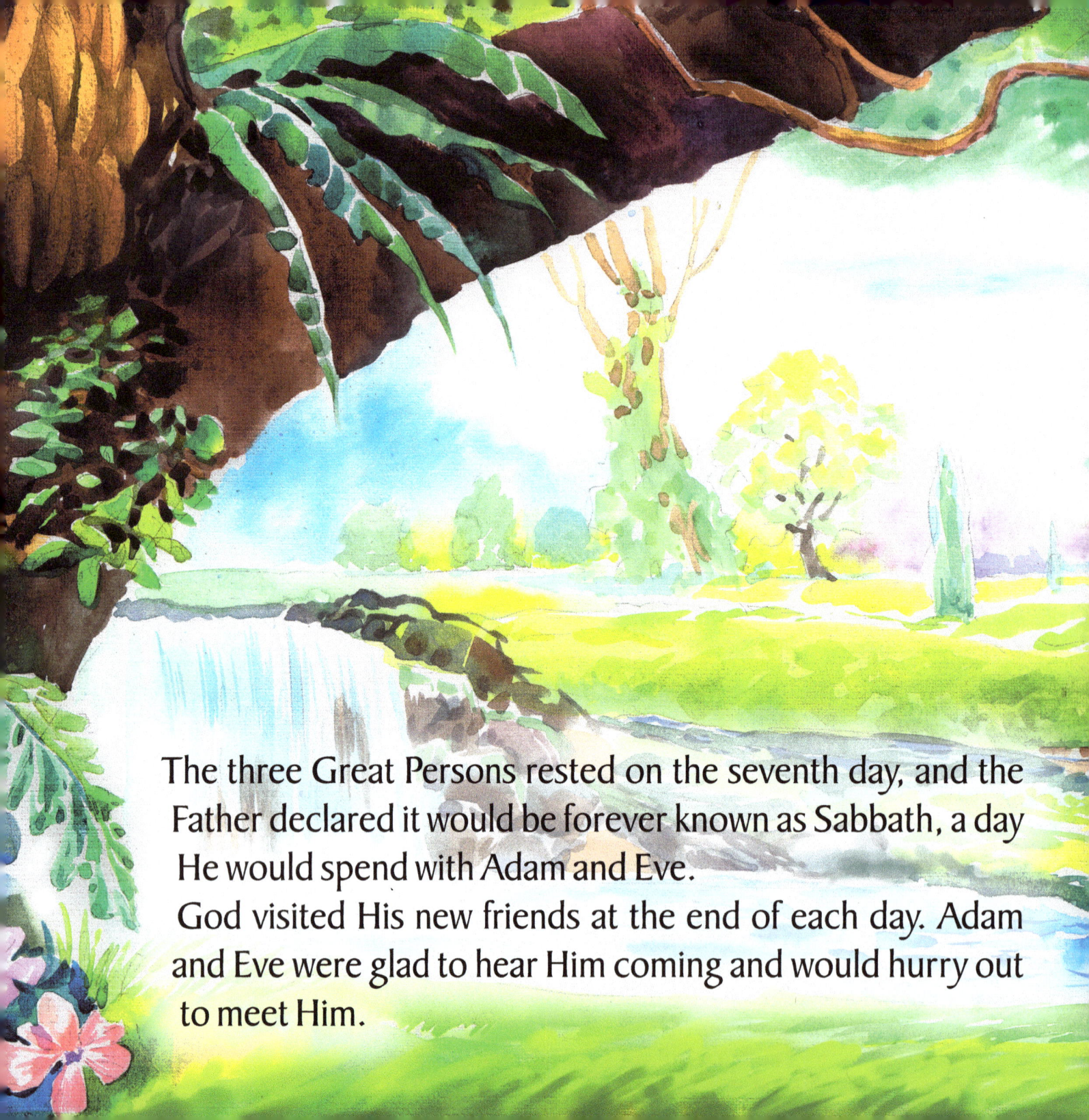

The three Great Persons rested on the seventh day, and the Father declared it would be forever known as Sabbath, a day He would spend with Adam and Eve.

God visited His new friends at the end of each day. Adam and Eve were glad to hear Him coming and would hurry out to meet Him.

The Father had planted two trees in the garden of Eden—the Tree of Life and the Tree of Knowledge of Good and Evil. God told Adam and Eve to eat as much as they wanted of the Tree of Life but to stay far away from the Tree of Knowledge of Good and Evil. He told them if they ate from it they would die. Adam and Eve promised to stay away from that tree because they loved God very much and wanted to obey Him.

One day as Eve walked alone in the Garden, she came by the forbidden tree. A beautiful serpent spoke to her and tempted her to eat the forbidden fruit. He lied and said, "You will not die."

Eve disobeyed God and hurried to Adam to give him the forbidden fruit. Adam was afraid, but he also disobeyed God. He took the fruit and quickly ate it.

One evening when God went to visit Adam and Eve, they did not come to meet Him. He looked for them and called, "Where are you?" Then Adam answered and said, "We hid because we are afraid." God asked, "Why are you afraid? Did you eat from the forbidden tree?" Adam told God how Satan had tricked them into eating from the forbidden tree.

The Father told Adam and Eve that they would need to leave their lovely home in Eden and the Tree of Life because they had disobeyed Him. The Son quickly stepped between the Father and Adam and Eve and offered to die in their place so Adam and Eve did not have to die that very day.

The Son said He would come back to Earth as a human, just like Adam and Eve. He would live a life without sin and die in their place so that they wouldn't have to. Adam and Eve felt sad that they had to leave their special home, but they had hope that someday soon they would see God again.

God walked with Adam and Eve down the pathway and through the gates of Eden. It was a tearful time, but they knew that someday in the future the Son would sacrifice His life for them, giving them a second chance.

Outside the gates of Eden, God gave Eve a hug and threw his arms around Adam. Then God said, "Good-bye." Two angels with flaming swords were sent to guard the gate of Eden and the way to the Tree of Life.

The Son returned to Orion to be with the Father and the Holy Spirit. They all wept together. This was the beginning of God's sadness for Planet Earth.

The Three Great Persons were looking forward to the day when the Son would be born as Baby Jesus on Earth to save the people. When that day came, it would come to be celebrated as Christmas all over the world.

We invite you to view the complete
selection of titles we publish at:
www.TEACHServices.com

We encourage you to write us
with your thoughts about this,
or any other book we publish at:
info@TEACHServices.com

TEACH Services' titles may be purchased in
bulk quantities for educational, fund-raising,
business, or promotional use.
bulksales@TEACHServices.com

Finally, if you are interested in seeing
your own book in print, please contact us at:
publishing@TEACHServices.com

We are happy to review your manuscript at no charge.

www.ingramcontent.com/pod-product-compliance
Lightning Source LLC
Chambersburg PA
CBHW042024180426
43200CB00034B/2995